KU-175-491

Questions!
Questions!

Questions! Questions!

by John Marshall

Illustrated by Kevin Wade

You choose the answers
You read this book your way

Dedicated to Susie and Lisa and all the children who have asked me so many questions over the last twenty years.

Many thanks to Helen for typing and retyping my words. Also to Elrose for such creative editing.

First published 1995
Reprinted 1997

Scripture Union, 207-209 Queensway
Bletchley, Milton Keynes, MK2 2EB

ISBN 0 86201 955 9

British Library Cataloguing-in-Publication Data.
A catalogue record for this book is available from the British Library.

Designed by Tony Cantale Graphics

Printed and bound in Great Britain by
Cox & Wyman Ltd, Reading, Berkshire

Usually people skip this bit of a book, but you need to read it because this book is very different;

At the bottom of most pages there is a box. Some of them have arrows by them, while others have a question mark. If there is an arrow the box tells you which page to turn to... but if there is a question mark you have to be brave enough to make a decision - and then follow to the page of your choice. There are so many different ways to read this book - you decide which way to go.

On many pages there is a Bible bit. If you want to check out the verses for yourself you will need a Bible. All the Bible bits in this book are from the Good News Bible - but if you have another modern translation (like the New International Version) it will be very similar. If you find it difficult to use a Bible there is usually an index in the front that will help you.

You will need a bookmark!

Do you remember when you were first learning to read in school? Your teacher used to mark off the pages you had read on a bookmark. (It was often an old Christmas card!)

Because this book involves a lot of jumping from one page to another, we thought that a marker like that would be a good idea, so we have provided one inside the front cover.

You can circle the numbers as you read the pages. You might even link the circles to show the route you've chosen - like this:

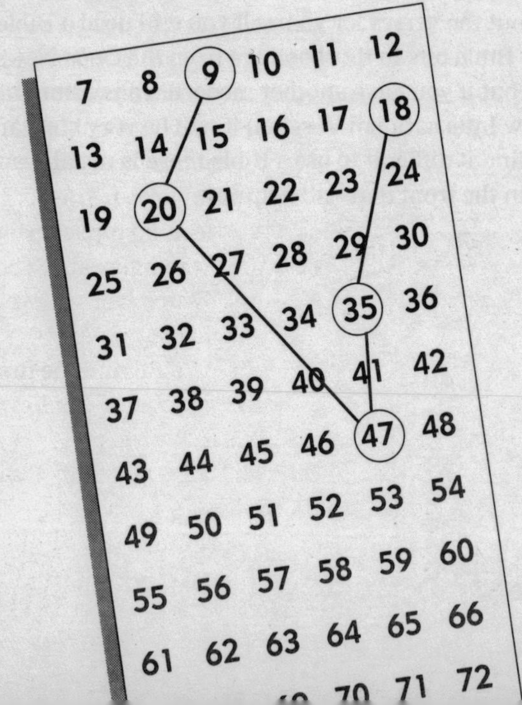

How to plan a journey

A friend of mine has a computer program which he uses whenever he goes on a car journey. Steve tells the computer where he is starting from and where he is going to. The computer then gives him three different routes. There's the quickest one, the shortest one and one that avoids motorways. I suppose it could be programmed to give other routes too: the one with the best scenery, the longest route, one that avoids roundabouts... the list could go on.

There are lots of different routes through this book! You may find the shortest - or the longest. If you choose only one route you will miss thinking about some very important big questions. You may want to read the book several times using different routes. You might want to check your bookmark to see which pages you haven't read. You could look up topics using the index at the end. Whichever way you choose, have fun.

You'll find the first decision after you have read page 9. Have a great adventure. I'll see you at the other end of the book!!

Questions, Questions

The world is full of questions.

- Why can't I stop up late?
- How does a CD work?
- What can you get for only £1.00 a week pocket money?
- Where does the soap go in the bath?

Some questions are BIG... others quite small. Here are some huge questions. Which is the most important to you?

1. **Who am I?** I know my name and address, but who am I? Why am I here? Am I special?
2. **Why is the world a mess?** Will it last? Can we protect all the whales and elephants? Will wars ever end? Who will plug the holes in the ozone layer?
3. **Are all religions true?** As well as Christianity we learn about other religions such as Islam and Buddhism. How do I know where truth is?
4. **Why should I read this book?** I'd prefer to watch TV or defend the universe on my computer.

Not an easy choice, is it?

- If you think 1 is the most important progress to page **10**.
- If you think 2 is, progress to page **20**.
- If it's 3 - page **28**.
- If it's 4 - page **44**.

10 Who am I?

Some answers are easy:

- How old are you?
- When's your birthday?
- Who's in your family?
- What school do you go to?
- What's your favourite food/TV programme/lesson at school?
- Have you any hobbies?
- Who are your friends? ... and so on...

All these facts begin to answer the big question: Who am I? But other bits of the answer are harder:

- Where do I belong?
- Why am I alive?
- Am I special?

TO HELP US EXPLORE FURTHER - WE NEED TO ANSWER ANOTHER QUESTION!

Here it is: **Am I important?**

What is your answer?

- **If your answer to that last question is yes, turn to page 24.**
- **If your answer is no or not sure - turn to page 39.**

Trying to win the battle

God is good. Sometimes we know we're not up to his standard. It's like the battle between good and bad. We want to be God's friend - but somehow the wrong in us has to be defeated.

Over the years many people have suggested many answers to deal with the things that spoil us.

Doing good: It's right that we should want to help others and always do what is right. But there is a big difference between doing good and being good. The first one can't replace the second.

Going to church: This is a particular example of doing good. It's a great idea to go - and enjoy the activities - but on its own it won't make us different. If you go and sit in a hen house you don't become a chicken. Just by sitting in church we don't become friends of God.

Comparing ourselves with others and thinking that we're better than they are: Now this only works if you choose someone who is worse than you. The person we should compare ourselves to is Jesus - but then we realise how far short of God's standard we fall.

There seems no way to win this war. Only one person, Jesus, has ever won the battle between good and evil. Christians believe he's the only one who can help us.

• Page **29** tells us more. Turn to it now.

Why read the Bible?

If the Bible really is God's book, then all it contains is true. We have to try and understand it.

What is the true God like? Can I know him? Does he care about me?

If we can answer the first question, then the others will begin to slot into place.

The Bible says that if you want to know what God is like then you must take a long look at Jesus, because when Jesus came to earth it was God walking around. Here's some Bible bits:

"Christ is the visible likeness of the invisible God." *Colossians 1:15*

"He (Jesus) is the exact likeness of God's own being." *Hebrews 1:3*

Jesus himself made the same claims:

"Whoever has seen me has seen the Father." *John 14:9*

So, for example, when we want to make sense of other religions we have to see how they deal with this very special person, Jesus.

To do this we need to know more about this person.

• Turn to page 16 to find out more.

Someone thinks you are special

Hold on to your hat, because here's something incredible. The most important person in the universe loves you. He's more important than the Prime Minister, the Royal Family and even the President of the United States. It's God, and the Bible tells us that God loves us and he has actually chosen us.

He chose to make us - and used himself as the model - so we are made like him.

He has chosen to need us. He actually loves us enough to care. He wants us to be his friends. Any friend of the Royal Family is treated as important. How much more special to be God's friend! God takes it even further and wants us to be part of his family.

To begin to understand how special we are, we need to discover a bit more about God.

• Start by turning to page **35**.

Who did Jesus claim to be?

Jesus claimed to be God. He could have been trying to trick everyone. That would make him a liar. When we begin to read his story in the Bible, the person we meet is not a deceiver.

It is always important to see if what a person says agrees with how they live. Jesus told others always to live truthfully. If he wasn't God, he would have been living one big lie. In one Bible bit Jesus actually said:

"The truth will set you free." *John 8:32*

Working with him for over three years, Jesus' close friends, the disciples, would have discovered the truth. If he had been lying they would have left him. Instead he became the most important person in their lives. Years after he was no longer on earth, some of them were prepared to die because they were his followers. Jesus has continued to be the greatest source of love for people ever since. But liars are usually selfish people. And then there's his death. Imagine you were tricking people, and because of it you faced death. You would own up to the authorities, try to make a deal with them or negotiate a compromise. Yet Jesus did none of this. As his arrest came nearer, he calmly predicted his coming to life again. The evidence suggests Jesus was not lying. That leaves two options.

- If you think he was mad turn to page **19**.
- If he really was God-on-earth turn to page **27**.

God is great and powerful

David, who was an Old Testament king himself, describes God in this Bible bit:

"You are great and powerful, glorious, splendid and majestic. Everything in heaven and earth is yours and you are king, supreme ruler over all." *1 Chronicles 29:11*

It's enough to frighten anyone! I can't imagine meeting the King of Kings and not being nervous.

- However clean our clothes were, we would feel scruffy.
- However good our lives are, we would feel unworthy and even guilty. Partly this is because we've been ignoring God, or even rebelling against him.
- He wants us to tell the truth, but often lies are easier.
- He wants us to share what we have, yet so often we are selfish.
- He wants us to be friends with other people, but sometimes we're horrible to them.

The list could go on and on. The Bible has one short word for all this activity: SIN. Until we do something about sin in our lives we will always feel this mixture of fear and guilt. When we think about God it makes us very uncomfortable.

- If you think something needs to be done about the sin in our lives, turn to page **25**.
- If you disagree or are not sure turn to page **26**.

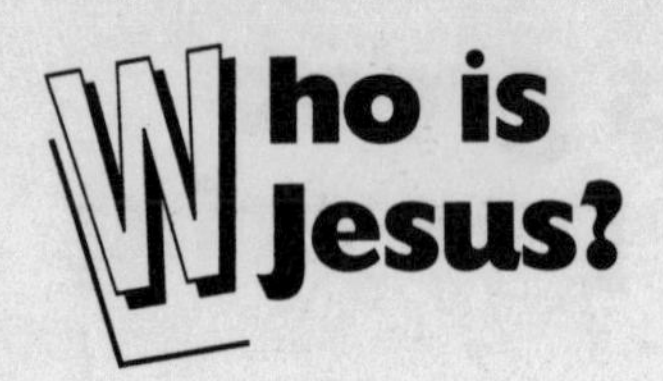

Who is Jesus?

It seems that every year the world stops for a holiday at Christmas, when we remember the birth of Jesus.

We basically date our calendar from his birth too.

Jesus, then, walked on earth about two thousand years ago. Millions of people claim that Christ has made an enormous difference to their lives. So who is Jesus?

According to the Bible, Jesus was born in Bethlehem but he grew up in Nazareth (both in modern Israel). He was given the name Jesus by an angel who announced his miraculous birth to his mother Mary. She had never had sexual intercourse. God's Holy Spirit had created the baby in her womb.

As he grew up, Jesus helped his earthly father Joseph, who was a carpenter. When he was about thirty years old, Jesus started travelling and teaching, loving, helping and healing people. The four books in the Bible that tell his life story are called the Gospels. They are Matthew, Mark, Luke and John.

Jesus healed sick people, gave sight to the blind, enabled lame men to walk and even brought back to life people who were dead. Jesus did many miracles. Thousands flocked to hear his teaching.

Inevitably that means he had enemies, who were jealous of his popularity. They wanted to destroy him. And after three years of doing good, Jesus was arrested, tried and killed by being nailed to a cross.

The Bible story doesn't end there because just three days later his tomb was found to be empty. He had come back to life, and many people saw him in the forty days before he went back to heaven. Some even touched his body.

It was this resurrection that finally convinced some of his friends that Jesus really was God. One of them, Thomas, doubted until he met the risen Jesus. After Jesus had spoken to him, Thomas answered:

"My Lord and My God." *John 20:28*

Jesus himself claimed to be God.

• Either turn to page **38** to discover what he said.
• Or go to page **88** to read more about Jesus' miracles.

Can God be a king and a friend?

So far we've discovered that God is both almighty (All Mighty) and that he wants to be our friend. We would like to meet him.

It is difficult to imagine what God would look like; the Bible uses lots of different pictures. Here are two:

King. If we were to meet a member of the Royal Family we would feel very nervous. We couldn't relax. We might feel awkward. Sometimes it's like that when we know God is speaking to us.

Friend. It's very different with friends. It is fun. We enjoy being with them and talking to them.

Right now, do you imagine God more as a friend or as a king?

• Turn to page **15** if your answer is a king to be feared.
• And turn to page **30** if it is a friend to be enjoyed.

Jesus was God-on-earth

Jesus claimed to be God-on-earth. If he was wrong, but did not realise it, he would have been mentally ill. Was Jesus mad?
Here's a few facts to prove he could not have been insane:
1. As soon as you start to read his story in the Bible the person you meet in the pages is not a mad or sad one, but a strong one.
2. Importantly, as we think about this question, Jesus has incredible intelligence. His teachings are still studied because they are so deep. The greatest professors of philosophy in the world can still find new ideas within them. Such teaching cannot come from someone who is mentally disturbed.
3. Jesus never rushed around madly. He was always calm and in control. Whether he was caught in a storm at sea, debating with religious leaders or on trial for his life, Jesus always had authority. He was never impatient or in a rush.

We've just used words like deep, calm and in control. These are not words to describe a madman, although they do accurately describe Jesus. So we're left with two options.

• If you think he was trying to trick everyone turn to page **14**.
• If he really was God-on-earth turn to page **27**.

Why is the world in a mess?

Every day the newspapers and TV bulletins remind us of famines, wars, natural disasters and terrorist attacks. There's a growing list of animals (like rhinos and whales) in danger of extinction, mainly because of hunting. The environment needs protection, or all the rain forests will be destroyed and acid rain will pollute more and more lakes.

Was it always like this?

Behind everything that is made there is a designer and maker. The Bible shows that God is the one who planned and created the world. The very first part of the very first book in the Bible (Genesis) teaches this. Here's a Bible bit that gives God's opinion of the world he made:

"God looked at everything he had made and was very pleased." *Genesis 1:31*

But he can't be pleased with the state of the world today, so we need to ask another big question.

What causes the problems?

The answer is very complex. One part of the answer occurs over and over again: OUR SELFISHNESS and DISOBEDIENCE.

From the beginning God made rules for people to follow. If they had obeyed, the world would have continued as he wanted it to. Instead they ignored the rules and did what they wanted to. They acted selfishly.

It's the same for us. That's what causes fights in our homes. One person will grab the TV controls and say, "I want the football." Someone else will join in, "I hate football. I want pop music." The first person says, "I was here first..." and soon an argument or fight starts. If only we could share. It's the same in the world.

- There is enough food for everyone. Some of us (because we are too selfish) take more than our fair share.
- At least one side fighting in a war wants more land or power because it is selfish - and tries to grab it from the other.
- Rain forests are destroyed because some people want more land to graze more cattle.
- Whales are hunted because some people want to eat their meat.

This Bible bit makes the same point:

"Where do all the fights and quarrels among you come from? You want things but you cannot have them, so you are ready to kill."
James 4:1-2

Dealing with selfishness

If we could all stop being greedy, there's no doubt the world would improve.

- If you think we can deal with our selfishness turn to page **63**.
- If you think we need help go to page **47**.

How did Jesus' death happen?

The night before Jesus died, he had a last meal with his friends. During the meal Jesus took some bread, broke it and said it was like his body. Jesus said he had to die so that they could be forgiven.

Then he passed round a cup of wine. He said this was like his blood (that is his life). It had to be poured out so that a new start could be made. (Whenever a church has a communion service it is remembering this meal.) During the meal, Judas (one of his disciples) sneaked off to betray Jesus by showing the Roman soldiers and temple guards where Jesus could be arrested quietly.

Jesus' first trial was in front of the religious leaders, who were jealous of Jesus and wanted him dead. His second was with the Roman Government official, Pontius Pilate, who had the power to kill him although he knew Jesus had done nothing to deserve death. Because Pilate was a coward, he gave in to the religious leaders and agreed that Jesus could be beaten, mocked and then killed. He was executed on a hill (sometimes called Golgotha or Calvary) outside the city of Jerusalem. He was nailed through his wrists and ankles to a huge cross of wood. Three people were executed that Friday. We now remember it as Good Friday. It seems strange to call the day that Jesus died 'good', doesn't it? Can you think why it has been given that name?

You can read the whole story in much more detail in any of the four gospels:

- Matthew 26:14 to 27:66
- Mark 14:10 to 15:47
- Luke 22:1 to 23:56
- John 18:1 to 19:42

When Jesus died it looked as if he had been defeated but that's not the end of the story.

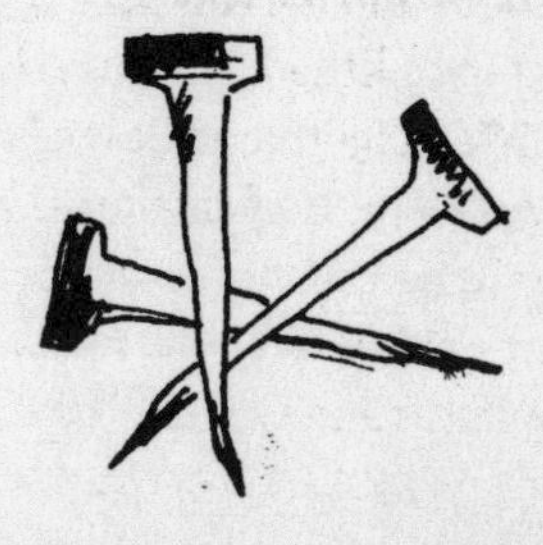

• Turn to page **48** to discover if his death was a mistake. (I think it gives some clues to why the day is called Good Friday.)

Why am I important?

When people ask us why we're important or special the answer will be something like:

- I'm the oldest in my family.
- I am a librarian at school.
- My Aunty asked me to be a bridesmaid/page boy at her wedding.
- I am captain of the rounders team.
- I was once rushed to hospital, and the ambulance even used its blue flashing light and siren when it jumped the traffic lights in the town centre.

Stop for a moment and look at these answers. They all involve other people: family, friends, teachers.

- Sometimes asking you to do things.
- Sometimes looking to you as leader.
- Sometimes just showing love to you.

The reason we think we are important is because we are special to others. There's another important reason why we are all special.

• Turn to page 13 to find out.

Hunting for forgiveness

Have you ever been on a treasure hunt? You search high and low... following clues only to discover that someone else has got to the end first and is now eating chocolate by the fistful!

If we are really serious about dealing with our sin (ignoring God and rebelling against him) we need to go on a hunt for forgiveness. Only when he's forgiven us can we start a friendship with him again.

The Bible is a bit like a treasure hunt. If we search in it we will find answers...

• Turn to page 33 to discover what sort of book the Bible is.

Why do we need to deal with sin?

Have you heard of Admiral Nelson, the famous British sailor who led the British navy in the wars against the French about two hundred years ago? After one battle which the British won, the French admiral came to Nelson's battleship to surrender. Nelson turned his back on the man. He would not shake his hand or make friends until the Frenchman took off the sword he was wearing and gave it up to the British.

It's the same for us. We can't make friends with people who still want to fight us.

It's the same for God. He can't be our friend if we keep sinning.

Sin is a bit like the French admiral's sword. Nelson only knew he was genuinely interested in peace when the weapon was no longer worn.

We show we are serious about being friends with God when we want our sins dealt with. That's why Christians talk a lot about forgiveness.

It's time to go on a treasure hunt for forgiveness.

• There's a clue on page **25**.

Was Jesus really God?

Jesus certainly claimed to be "God-on-earth."

When we begin to read his story in the Bible the facts seem to agree. God must always be perfect and Jesus never did anything wrong. He never had to say sorry and ask for forgiveness. His close friends, Peter and John, both mention this in the Bible bits they wrote:

"There is no sin in him." *1 John 3:5*

"He committed no sin and no one ever heard a lie come from his lips." *1 Peter 2:22*

Both friends knew Jesus was different. They had never heard anyone teach like Jesus. They had never seen anyone perform miracles like Jesus. What they couldn't know is that the influence of Jesus today would be stronger than it was when he was on earth two thousand years ago.

If Jesus was God, he could not stay dead. God's power is stronger than death. Jesus would have to be alive. For many people this is the final convincing proof that Jesus was "God-on-earth". He came back to life just three days after he was killed.

To discover how all this happened, we have to start with his death.

• Let's turn to page **22** to do that.

What about other religions?

Most probably at school you've learnt not only about Christianity but also about other religions. Which of these have you heard of?

- Islam
- Hinduism
- Judaism
- Buddhism
- Sikhism

You may have friends who belong to another faith. Some people will say that all religions help us find God. Others disagree. It is very difficult to know what is true Perhaps the right question to ask is: "Has God spoken?" If he has, he will have shown us the truth.

Christians believe that as God loves us he doesn't want to tease us (or hurt us) by hiding himself. He has spoken, and the Bible is a written record of what he has said. Here's a Bible bit that says just that:

"In the past God spoke to our ancestors many times and in many ways through the prophets." *Hebrews 1:1*

What we have to decide is whether we believe that the Bible truly is God's book.

- If you think it is turn to page **12**.
- If you are not sure go to page **50**.

Where does evil come from?

Much of Jesus' life was a battle between good and evil. When he was a baby the evil King Herod tried to kill him. Before he started to teach, he was tempted by the devil in the desert. We remember this in Lent, the forty days before Easter.

Jesus recognised that the devil was the starting point for all evil.

Who is the devil?

The Bible says that one very important angel started to feel he was more important than God. He became so proud he even thought he could replace God. Because of this, God had to expel Satan (another name for the devil) from heaven. The devil is the very opposite of Jesus.

- Jesus is the truth - the devil is a liar
- Jesus is good - the devil is evil
- Jesus has all power - the devil's power is limited

When Jesus died on the cross, it *seemed* that the battle between good and evil had been won by evil. That's why the fact that Jesus came back from the dead is so important. It is called the resurrection. The devil had done his worst but Jesus beat him.

God's power was stronger than the devil's.

• Turn to page 36 to find out more about Jesus coming back from the dead.

Who are Jesus' friends?

I guess you've got some good friends at school. We use
to have lots of Johns in my class, so nicknames had to
be invented to save confusion. "Cherry" Orchard's re
name was John. John Porter became "Potty" and I wa
"Dillon", named after a marshal in a TV cowboy
programme.

When Jesus was on earth he made friends. There
were the twelve disciples. Within this group there we
three special friends: James, John and Peter. He had
other friends too. All the time he was showing people
that God wants friendship with us.

This Bible bit is actually the words of Jesus himsel

"You are my friends if you do what I command you... I call you friends, because I have told you everything I have heard from the Father..." *John 15:14,15*

Friends get to know each other well. If we want to
friends with God we need to discover more about Jes

• If you want to start by finding out what hi name means turn to page **95**.
• If you want to answer the question 'Who i Jesus?' go to page **16**.

God speaks through his creation

I remember years ago using a chairlift to go up a high mountain in Switzerland. The scenery was beautiful. In the valley it was bright summer sun. Then we went up into the snow. All around there was silence. It was wonderful. When we look at any beautiful view like that we learn something of the God who created it. We discover he is creator, that he is caring, beautiful, majestic and magnificent. God speaks through our world. This Bible bit was written as a poem by someone who had seen something of God in creation.

"How clearly the sky reveals God's glory!
How plainly it shows what he has done!
Each day announces it to the following day;
Each night repeats it to the next.
No speech or words are used
no sound is heard
yet their voice goes out to all the world."
Psalm 19:1-4

God speaks through other people

There are some people who it is good news to be with. They are fun - always doing and saying things that spark us. When we meet people we learn something of God. He makes each of us unique. God speaks through other people. This often happens when we are at church.

Once God came and lived on earth as a person. As we discover more about Jesus we discover that God is actually speaking to us - loud and clear.

• Turn to page 16 to do that.

What is the Bible?

Part of the answer is easy. The Bible is like a whole library in one volume. It is made up of 66 books. The Old Testament has 39, which leaves 27 in the New Testament. These were written by a whole variety of people including kings, shepherds, a tax officer, a tent-maker and a doctor. Some of these lived hundreds of years before Jesus was born. Others were his friends when he lived on earth. The Old Testament starts with the world being created and goes on to describe what happened to God's people, the Israelites, before Jesus was born.

The New Testament starts with the story of Jesus and tells what happened to his early followers. Parts of the Bible are history, others are poems or letters. Some parts are easier to understand than others. God gives his laws in some books, while others are prophecy where God speaks out against evil.

The original books of the Bible were not written in English. The Old Testament was generally written in Hebrew (with a few parts in Aramaic). The New Testament was mainly written in Greek. That's why there are now different English Bibles, because different groups of people have had a go at translation.

But the Bible makes a bigger claim for itself. It claims to be God's book. When the writers were at work, God actually influenced them in such a way that they wrote down his thoughts. Now through these words he speaks to us hundreds of years later.

One Bible bit says:

"All Scripture is inspired by God."

2 Timothy 3:16

• If you know that the Bible is God's book turn to page **12**.
• If you're not sure what to believe about the Bible turn to page **87**.
• If you want to discover more about the Old Testament turn to page **80**.
• If you want to read more about the New Testament go to page **78**.

What's God like?

Do you like learning new words - especially long ones? Here's some that all start with OMNI (Latin for "all"; many of our English words come from Latin):

- OMNIPOTENT: (pronounced OM-NIP-PO-TENT) All-powerful
- OMNIPRESENT:(OM-NE-PRE-SENT) Always present
- OMNISCIENT: (OM-NIS-CE-ENT) All knowing

All three words can be used about God. He is omnipotent because he's all powerful. He created the universe. He's always with us - so he's omnipresent. He knows everything - so he is omniscient.

It means he knows everything about us. Psalm 139 is all about God's omniscience and omnipresence. Here are some bits:

"Lord...you know me."

"You know everything I do..."

"You know all my actions..."

"You are around me on every side."

All this means we can't keep secrets from God! Knowing all that about him, is God the type of person you would like to meet?

- If you would like to meet God turn to page **18**.
- If you would be frightened to meet him turn to Page **15**.
- If you are not sure if God exists go to page **90**.

What happened after Jesus died?

Jesus died on a Friday. His body was placed in a cave tomb belonging to a rich man called Joseph of Arimathea. A huge stone was used to seal the entrance. His enemies arranged for soldiers to guard the tomb.

Nobody came on the Saturday because it was the Jewish rest day, called the Sabbath.

On Sunday morning some friends of Jesus came to the garden where the cave was. They found the stone had been moved and Jesus' body had disappeared. Angels, God's messengers, said that he was alive again! Jesus' friends could hardly believe it, but during that day many of them met the risen Jesus.

One friend, Mary, spoke to him before she left the garden that morning. At some time during the day Peter and Jesus had a meeting. In the afternoon two of Jesus' followers walked almost seven miles with him to a village before realising who was travelling with them. In the evening most of his disciples met him in an upstairs room where they had a meal together.

Over the next forty days hundreds of people saw Jesus and discovered that he had come back from the dead. His enemies tried to stop the facts from spreading. They bribed the guards from the tomb to say that Jesus' body had been stolen by the disciples.

After forty days Jesus returned to heaven. He never died again. He spoke with the disciples on a hill in

Galilee for one last time.

Here's how one Bible bit describes what happened:

"He was taken up to heaven as they (the disciples) watched him and a cloud hid him from their sight." *Acts 1:9*

This event is called the Ascension.

You can actually read the full story of Jesus coming back from the dead – his resurrection – in these Bible bits:

- Matthew 28
- Mark 16
- Luke 24
- John 20 and 21

Today some people are still not sure whether they believe Jesus came alive again, while others are convinced.

• If you want to discover more evidence for the resurrection turn to page **40**.
• If you want to think about what Jesus being alive means to you, go to page **43**.

What did Jesus claim?

If a friend came into school one morning and claimed to be God everyone in the class would just laugh at him. But that's the startling claim that Jesus made about himself.

No other recognised religious leader has ever claimed to be God. Here are some Bible bits:

"The Father and I are one." *John 10:30*

"Believe in God and believe also in me." *John 14:1*

Jesus allowed people to worship him. He claimed to forgive people their sins (and only God can do that). His miracles were signs that he was God. After Jesus was arrested, at his trial, the high priest asked him, "Are you the Messiah, the Son of the blessed God? "'I am,' answered Jesus." *Mark 14:61-62*

Lots of people think that Jesus is just the best teacher who ever lived or the very best man ever. But by saying he was God, he is either someone much more or much less.

Either Jesus was telling the truth or he was trying to trick everyone, or he was mad. What do you think?

- If he was telling the truth turn to page **27**.
- If he was trying to trick everyone or you are not sure turn to page **14**.
- If he was mad turn to page **19**.

Can I be special?

Perhaps you've answered no or not sure because you've never done anything extra special like:

- Coming top in a class exam, (even if you've had work displayed in the local library).
- Representing the school in a sports team, (you did come second in an infants' sack race once).
- Winning Trivial Pursuits when playing against Grandad who can still remember when Britain was great (but don't ask him or he'll tell you again...and again...and again...).

Have you noticed every one of these answers - and the ones you are thinking of - are all about what other people think of you, or what you do with other people.

It seems that if others like and love you - you are special.

If no-one does - you feel unimportant.

But there is someone who loves us - and that makes us special.

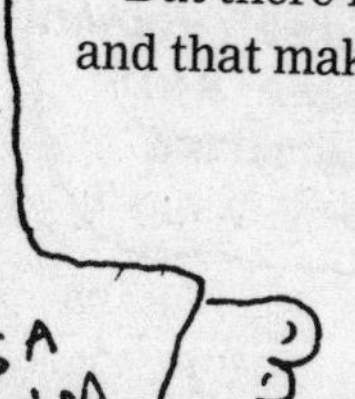

• Go on to page **13** to discover.

More evidence for the resurrection

1. We have already said that the tomb Jesus was placed in was found empty. If Jesus didn't come back from the dead, what could be the explanation?

Here are some suggestions:

• Jesus didn't die on the cross but only fainted, after being wounded by the nails and a soldier's spear. If this happened, could a very weak person move a huge stone door? Could he get past the guards? This doesn't make sense.

• Jesus' friends could have stolen the body and pretended he had come back to life. Again the huge

stone door and the guards would prevent this.

• Jesus' enemies could have stolen the body, but the last thing they wanted was for people to believe Jesus had risen. If they had stolen it - when the resurrection story was spreading - they would have admitted it and perhaps even shown everybody the dead body. The only explanation is that Jesus came back from the dead.

2. Jesus showed himself to lots of people. He ate fish with his disciples, and allowed them to touch him. He was not a ghost!

3. Just a few months after the resurrection, the Christian church came into being. As Paul says in this Bible bit:

> **"If Christ has not been raised from death then we have nothing to preach and you have nothing to believe."** *1 Corinthians 15:14*

4. The disciples were completely changed after meeting the risen Lord Jesus. They had been afraid and timid but soon they were brave enough to preach to thousands of people. They were persecuted for believing. Some were even killed. No one dies for something they don't believe to be true.

5. Through the two thousand years since, the Christian church has grown. Millions of people have had their lives changed once they've accepted that Jesus is their Lord.

• Turn to page **43** to see what Jesus being alive will mean to us.

What is hell like?

One thing is clear from Jesus' teaching about hell: it is total separation from God. In a story he told, there is:

"...a deep pit (between heaven and hell) so that those who want to cross over...cannot do so." *Luke 16:26*

This means that there is no contact with God at all. In hell there can be no love or healing or friendship or life, as these are all gifts that come only from God.

God turns his back on people who have chosen to turn their backs on him.

A Bible bit talks about the Lord Jesus as judge coming:

"To punish those who reject God and who do not obey the Good News about the Lord Jesus. They will suffer the punishment of eternal destruction, separated from the presence of the Lord..." *2 Thessalonians 1:8,9*

All this can be frightening. But remember that one result of Jesus' resurrection was that we can know his love.

• Turn to page **64** if you want to discover more about God's love.
• If you want to look at the links between Jesus' resurrection and us today, turn to page 43.

What does Jesus' resurrection mean to me?

Jesus is still alive. He is now King of Kings in heaven but he has not changed. Here's a Bible bit that says that:

"Jesus Christ is the same yesterday, today and forever." *Hebrews 13:8*

This fact should change the way we think about many things. Here are some of them:

1. Because Jesus is alive someone really does listen when we pray.

2. Because Jesus is alive there really is life after death.

3. Because Jesus is alive we know he was always telling the truth. That means one day he will come back to the earth just as he promised.

4. Because Jesus is alive we can know his love and friendship for ourselves.

What a lot to discover!

• Turn to page **51** for some ideas about how to pray.

• Turn to page **53** if you want to think more about heaven, hell and life after death.

• Turn to page **61** if you would like to discover more about Jesus coming back to earth.

• Page **64** is all about how special we are because God loves us.

Why should I read this book?

Personally I reckon there are a number of reasons why you should have a good look through this book. Here's a few:

1. Someone has paid good money to buy the book. It may even have been you! If you don't read it you'll have wasted your own cash.
2. This book is unlike any other you've tried to read.
3. If you are honest, you do have some big questions and it would be good to find some answers.

• Now if you can't remember the other questions go back to page **9**.
• If you can then for Question 1 go to page **10**.
• Question 2 - page **20**.
• Question 3 - page **28**.

Am I ready to say 'yes' to Jesus?

Here is one of the most famous bits in the whole Bible:

"For God loved the world so much that he gave his only son, that everyone who believes in him may have eternal life." *John 3:16*

Eternal means going on for ever and ever. The only life like that is God's life. God loves us so much he actually wants us to share his life. To do that, we have to believe. That means we really do trust that Jesus was God-on-earth; he really did die for all our wrong; he really is alive; and he really can make us the type of people he wants us to be.

A Christian is someone who has said 'yes' to Jesus, someone who wants him to be boss in their lives.

You may already be a Christian - or you may be considering it right now. Before deciding whether or not we want to be followers of Jesus, it is important to work out what this will mean.

Here's a list of some of the responsibilities. You will need to check out all of them.

1. Living as a Christian - and doing what God wants.
2. Caring for the world around us.
3. Being part of the church.
4. Praying.
5. Getting to know Jesus better by Bible reading.

As you read these pages please remember two things:

• We don't have to become *good* to be a Christian. After we have said 'yes' to Jesus he will begin to help us change.

• It's actually having the faith to say 'yes' to Jesus that makes us Christians.

There's a Bible bit that says:

"It is by God's grace that you have been saved through faith. It is not the result of your own efforts, but God's gift so that no one can boast about it." *Ephesians 2:9*

Now choose which one of the list you are going to check first. Keep coming back to this point until you've checked all five routes. They are all important.

• Number One, turn to page **55**.
• Number Two, turn to page **65**.
• Number Three, turn to page **56**.
• Number Four, turn to page **69**.
• Number Five, turn to page **70**.

Can people change?

The Bible is full of stories about people who were changed. A well-known one is Zacchaeus who started off as a greedy cheat, but after he had met Jesus he changed into someone who could share.

The whole story is in Luke 19:1-10 but here's a Bible bit from the end.

"Zacchaeus stood up and said...I will give half my belongings to the poor." *Luke 19:8*

If everyone could become like that, the world would be a better planet. Christians believe that only God can help us change. So what's God like?

• Turn to Page **35** to start discovering.

Was Jesus' death a mistake?

Throughout the later part of his life Jesus kept saying he would die, but rise again from the dead. Here's a Bible bit from Matthew with Jesus' words:

"I must go to Jerusalem and suffer much...I will be put to death but three days later I will be raised to life." *Matthew 16:21*

It was obviously part of God's plan that Jesus should die. But why?

Before Jesus came to earth, when anyone wanted to be forgiven for their sin they had to sacrifice a lamb on an altar. God gave this instruction in Old Testament times. When Jesus came, John (the one who baptised Jesus) pointed Jesus out to some friends and said:

"There is the *lamb of God* who takes away the sin of the world." *John 1:29*

Jesus came to give his life as one final complete sacrifice for all the wrong things each of us has ever done or ever will do. Never again would people need to make other sacrifices before they could be forgiven.

Big Battles

Sometimes we have a big battle inside us: Should we do what we know is right, or something which is wrong (but often easier)?

Someone in our street is different from us. Perhaps they are fatter or no good at sport or have a different coloured skin. One day we hurt them by saying something nasty about them. The battle inside starts.

Should we apologise - which is hard - or do we just laugh about it with other people - which will hurt our neighbour even more?

It's a battle between good and evil.

When Jesus died on the cross it was the biggest battle possible between Good and Evil. As Jesus hung on the cross he suffered for us. He took the punishment instead of us.

- If you want to discover more about this battle turn to page **29**.
- If you think you can win this battle yourself turn to page **11**.
- If you have questions about suffering in the world turn to page **81**.

Discovering the truth

There are some things we can work out with our brains or with a calculator or computer. A good example would be how to win a game of chess. We know the rules, so by thinking we can work out a solution. The other player will also be doing the same. Another example would be the different routes between towns mentioned on page 7.

But there are some things that cannot be worked out using just logical thinking. These are mysteries. The only way for us to discover the truth would be if someone else gave us the information.

One group of children once told me I couldn't come into their den until I used the password. I told them I didn't know what it was. They said "Guess." But where do you begin? There are hundreds of thousands of words in the English language (and they could have used another language!) Until someone whispered it in my ear I couldn't do anything. This type of fact has to be revealed to us. By just using our brains we'll never discover the truth about God. We need to have it revealed to us.

Christians believe God has shown us the truth. He has spoken in the Bible.

• Now turn to page **33** to discover more.

How can we pray?

One day Jesus' friends asked him just that question. He taught them how, partly by giving them a model prayer. You may know it. It's the one that starts "Our Father in heaven."

If you want to find it in the Bible, look at:

- Matthew 6:9-13
- Luke 11:2-4

Sometimes it is good to use words written by other people when we pray. You may have a useful book of prayers. At other times it is better to make up your own prayers using your own words. This may be difficult at first, so here's a guide.

Try to STOP and pray. We're going to use each letter of the word STOP in turn. Make sure your prayers are honest!

S - SORRY

We should apologise to God for all the times we must have made him sad. Wonderfully he forgives us - if we really mean what we say. Sometimes this type of prayer is called confession.

T - THANKS

God has given us so much to enjoy in our lives. We must stop and thank him. The list is endless - but here's a start. Homes, friends, family, schools, churches, food, warmth, games - and especially Jesus.

O - OTHERS

There will be people we know who are not as fortunate as us. They may be ill, or hurting, or poor, or sad. Pray for them. Remember anywhere in the news where there is a famine, a war, an earthquake or another disaster. Sometimes we call these prayers our intercessions.

P - PERSONAL PLEASE

We can pray for anything in our lives that we may want to share with God. It could be to do with our home, school, friends or just us personally.

Think of prayer as a conversation with a friend. It's important to STOP talking some of the time, because in the quiet Jesus may want to speak to us.

Because Jesus is alive, he hears our prayers. And it won't stop there, because he'll answer them as well - always in the best way, which is not always the way we expect!

• If you want to look up some of the other reasons why Jesus' resurrection is so important go back to page **43**.
• If you want to think more about his friendship with you go on to page **64**.

What happens when we die?

Because Jesus came back from the dead, we know that death is not the end. Jesus himself said much about both heaven and hell.

Before we think about what heaven is like, it is important to realise we only live one life. Some other religions teach that people come back and live again on earth. Christians do not believe in re-incarnation.

One Bible bit clearly says:

"Everyone must die once and after that be judged by God." *Hebrews 9:27*

Everyone who believes in Jesus has a place in heaven.

Where is heaven?

The Bible doesn't tell us where heaven is. One thing is made clear: it is where God is. In his famous prayer Jesus taught people to start:

"Our Father in heaven..." *Matthew 6:9*

When Jesus came to earth, he came from heaven. When his work here was finished he went back there. Sometimes we use other names for heaven like paradise or glory.

In this Bible bit Jesus is speaking to his friends about heaven:

"There are many rooms in my father's house and I am going to prepare a place for you." *John 14:2*

What is heaven like?

Because God is there everything that spoils life on earth is excluded. There is a Bible bit that says:

> **"There will be no more death, no more grief or crying or pain."** *Revelation 21:4*

• Turn on to page **42** if you want to discover what Jesus said about hell.
• If you want to look up some of the other reasons why Jesus' resurrection is so important turn back to page **43** to make a choice.

How can I please God?

Have you ever heard anyone say, "You've done so much for me. I am grateful. Is there anything I can do for you?"

When Christians recognise that Jesus has done so much for us, we will want to do things for him. We must make every effort to live the type of life that will please him. It won't be easy, but he will help us.

We've got to be the type of people who are:

- loving
- good news to be with
- patient
- kind
- humble

and that's only the start of the list!

Christians have to try to be truthful and always do what they know to be right. It is really difficult but God wants to give us the power to do it.

• Turn to page **59** to discover how he wants to help.
• Turn back to page **45** if there are more responsibilities you need to check.

What is the church?

When the word 'church' is mentioned most of us think of a building - but that's not the real church. The church is people, not bricks! We become God's building blocks for his church. One Bible bit says:

"Come as living stones and let yourselves be used in building the spiritual temple."
1 Peter 2:3

Many of us first saw something of Jesus' love in other people at church. Remember we made that discovery on page 31.

As Christians we become part of God's church. We all need each other. One stone will not make a building on its own!!

We worship together. We pray and care for each other. We're honest with each other. We learn from each other. We strengthen each other.

God has a place in his church for each of us. There are many different denominations like Methodist, Baptist, Church of England, Roman Catholic, United Reformed, Pentecostal, Free Churches, House Churches, the

Salvation Army and so on. No one has all the truth. We learn from each other. More and more, people in churches today are working together.

Working together is sometimes really difficult but God wants to give us the power to do it.

All churches believe that Jesus is God, that his death was in our place and that we become Christians by trusting him.

There are other organisations that look very much like a church but they are not Christians. These groups are called cults.

• Turn to page **59** to discover how Jesus wants to give us the strength to live his way.
• Turn back to page **45** if there are more responsibilities you need to check.
• Many churches think of baptism as a visible sign that you've joined the church. Turn to page **85** to find out more.
• If you want to find out more about cults turn to page **92**.

A prayer you can use

A prayer many people have found helpful in saying 'yes' to Jesus:

Father God,
I know I have done many wrong and selfish things.
I believe that Jesus died on the cross for me.
I am sorry for all my sin. Please forgive me.
I ask you to come into my life to be my friend and helper.
Fill me with your Holy Spirit.
Begin to make me the person you want me to be.
Help me to follow you for the rest of my life.
Amen.

Praying a prayer like this does not make us into people who will never do or say or think wrong again. It does mean that God has now forgiven us not because of our life but because of the perfect life and death of the Lord Jesus.

- If you now want to make up your own prayer go to page **75**.
- If you have used this one - and made it yours - go on to page **73**.

Who is the Holy Spirit?

Before agreeing to have a part in a school play it is important to discover what you will have to do.

Before saying 'yes' to Jesus we need to discover the responsibilities we will have as Christians. As we do, it seems an impossible task. But God has promised to help us.

There's a Bible bit where Paul says:

"I have the strength to face all conditions by the power that Christ gives me."

Philippians 4:13

When we say yes to Jesus he actually comes and lives in us, by the power of his Holy Spirit. He begins to change us into the people he wants us to be and strengthens us to do the things he wants from us.

Before Jesus died he promised that the Holy Spirit would come from God as our:

"...helper, who will stay with you for ever."

John 14:16

God's Holy Spirit is a person, but he cannot be seen. Just as Jesus was "God-with-us", so the Holy Spirit is "God-in-us." He teaches us all things and leads us in the truth.

Fifty days after Jesus' resurrection (at a time called Pentecost) God kept this promise and the Holy Spirit filled the disciples. The story is in Acts 2. There was a sound of rushing wind and what looked like flames touching the disciples. They had been frightened people but now they became enthusiastic for Jesus and began to tell a crowd of thousands about him. Many believed and followed Jesus. Pentecost became the start of the Church.

The Holy Spirit is God. Christians believe that God is a Trinity: three persons in one "Godhead".

He promises to help us become more like Jesus. The Bible speaks of our lives producing good things just like a fruit tree producing good fruit.

The Holy Spirit brings gifts from God for each of us so that we can build up his church.

• If you want to discover more about the Trinity turn to page **72**.
• If you want to read about the fruit of the Spirit go to page **66**.
• If you want to discover more about the gifts of the Spirit read page **84**.
• Or turn to page **67** and read about saying 'yes' to Jesus.

Is Jesus coming back to earth?

country shows it has chosen a new king or queen by
olding a coronation. The most important part of the
eremony is when the new monarch is crowned. When
esus returned to heaven at the ascension, there was a
oronation in glory. A Bible bit speaks of Jesus:

"...raised...to the highest place above and (given) the name that is greater than any other name." *Philippians 2:9*

This bit goes on to speak about how everyone on
arth will one day fall on their knees and realise that
esus Christ is Lord. This will happen when Jesus
omes back to the earth.

He often spoke of this event himself. Here are some
cts about the second coming of Jesus:

- No one knows when it will happen.
- It will happen in the same way as Jesus ascended to heaven.
- Everyone on earth will know when it happens.
- Jesus will be seen - not as a little baby, or a wandering preacher, but as King of Kings.

One of the most famous pieces in Handel's *Messiah* is
e Hallelujah chorus. It's all about the second coming.
he choir sing "Hallelujah, for the Lord God
nnipotent reigneth. The kingdom of this world is
ecome the kingdom of our Lord and of his Christ and
shall reign for ever and ever. King of Kings and Lord

of Lords, Hallelujah."

This is quoted from the Bible book of Revelation 19:
and 11:15.

As King, Jesus will also be judge. Those who follow him will become part of his new kingdom. His people will be with him forever.

• If you want to discover more about the second coming of Jesus turn to page **83**.
• If you want to check out other reasons why Jesus' resurrection is so important go back to page **43** and make a choice.

Why can't I change myself?

Iany of us try to change
very year! On New Year's
ay we make resolutions.
'hey are usually broken before
he end of January.

What were your resolutions
his year?

How long did they last?

Every year I used to promise myself I would keep a
iary for the year, and every year I never made it
eyond the end of January.

If everyone in the world resolved to be unselfish,
'hat would happen? It may be better for a little while
ut it could not possibly last long. Soon people would be
rguing and quarrelling again.

The prophet Jeremiah wrote about how impossible it
; to alter the way we are in this Bible bit:

"Can a leopard remove its spots? If it could then you that do evil could learn to do what is right." *Jeremiah 13:23*

We need help to become less selfish.

• Turn to page 47 to find out how people can change for the better.

Can we know God's love?

A few years after Jesus left the earth, a man called Saul persecuted Christians for their beliefs. One day the risen Jesus met him, and Saul changed so much he eve had to have a new name: Paul. He later wrote much of the New Testament. He knew personally what he was writing about in these Bible bits:

"God has shown us how much he loves us - it was while we were still sinners that Christ died for us." *Romans 5:8*

"We were God's enemies, but he made us his friends, by the death of his Son." *Romans 5:10*

When Jesus came alive again, God was showing that his love will go on and on forever, reaching people and making friends with them.

His love reaches as far as us. He wants to include us in his family.

We need not fear life or death or today or tomorrow because nothing can separate us from the love of someone who has beaten death. See Romans 8:38-39.

One of the most famous Bible bits is John 3:16. It is a about God's love for us. I think it was the first Bible bit ever learnt by heart.

• Turn to page **45** to discover what it says.

Caring for the world around us

Think about how much Jesus has cared for us. Now he wants us to care for others, and not just those people we know and like. It includes caring for people of other races, with other customs. It includes people who are hurting in this country and elsewhere. Jesus cares for us in spite of the times we hurt him. Now he even wants us to care for people when they are nasty to us.

This involves being patient with others, forgiving hem and trying to end arguments and fights. In one Bible bit Jesus told us to: **"love one another"** (John 5:12) and in another even to **"love your enemies"** Matthew 5:44).

As we begin to work together, then we must make a new kind of world. Christians should care for the earth and try to protect it.

Keep a finger in this page, but go back to page 20. As Christians, God wants us to help solve these huge problems. (Come back to this page when you have reminded yourself!)

All this is really difficult, but God wants to give us he power to do it.

• Turn to page **59** to discover how he wants to help us.
• Turn back to page **45** if there are more responsibilities you need to check.

What is the fruit of the Spirit?

Jesus talked about himself as a vine on which grapes grow (John 15). He said his followers are like branches. His Spirit is like the sap running from the vine into the branches. All together the vine, the sap and the branches will produce bunches of grapes. God's Holy Spirit produces bunches of good fruit in our lives. The most famous Bible bunch is in Galatians. God's Holy Spirit will produce in us:

"...love, joy, peace, patience, kindness, goodness, faithfulness, humility and self-control." *Galatians 5:22-23*

When people see these qualities in our lives they will notice we are different. And it's all because we've said 'yes' to Jesus.

Jesus pointed out that:

"You will know (people) by what they do. Thorn bushes do not bear grapes...A healthy tree bears good fruit." *Matthew 7:16-17*

• Now turn to page **67** to discover more about saying 'yes' to Jesus.

Saying 'yes' to Jesus

Saying 'yes to Jesus involves:

• Realising that although God wants us to be friends we have been ignoring him and living the wrong sort of life.

• Believing that Jesus really was "God-on-earth" and when he died it was as a punishment for our wrong.

• Asking the living Jesus to take us over so that we become the type of people he wants us to be by his Holy Spirit living in us. We will do all we can to live as we know he wants us to.

Christians use different phrases to explain saying 'yes' to Jesus. These include:

• Trusting in him
• Believing in him
• Having faith
• Being born again
• Opening your life (or heart) to Jesus
• Salvation

We need to say 'yes' in a prayer. You may want to make up your own. You may prefer first to look at one that someone else has written. You may not yet be ready to say 'yes' to Jesus.

• If you want to pray your own prayer turn to page **75**.
• If you want to read and use someone else's prayer go to page **58**.
• If you are not yet ready to say 'yes' to Jesus turn to page **76**.

What is God doing about suffering?

When people hurt and suffer we usually ask why does it happen. A few years ago I was ill and in hospital. People kept asking me, "Why has God let this happen?" I hadn't got an answer, but I could answer the question "What is God doing about this suffering?" There were lots of parts to the answer. Here are a few:

- He's giving me courage to be brave.
- He's giving the doctors understanding.
- He's giving me the patience to get better.
- He's helping other people to understand what I'm going through.
- He's giving me family and friends who will always love and care.

God is always there when people are suffering.

- He's challenging people to give more money so that charities can buy the food to feed the hungry.
- He's giving the rescuers the bravery and courage to risk their own lives as they help the trapped and injured.
- He's giving brave people the right words to speak out against injustice or prejudice or selfishness.

God understands the battle between good and evil.

• Turn to page **29** to see how Jesus was involved in this war.

Praying

If we want to stay friends with people we need to keep in touch with them. We chat to friends at school, or 'phone people we haven't seen. We may write a letter. It's a good way to make new friends too. I'd like to hear if you've enjoyed this book. Write to me at the Scripture Union address on page 70.

Prayer is the way we keep in touch with Jesus. Prayer does not come naturally. We need to learn how to do it. Look back to page 51 and check out the ideas there. (But then come back to this page!)

Many Christians find it is helpful to have a regular prayer time every day. It is usually first thing in the morning, or around bedtime. You'll have to discover when is the best time for you.

Making time to pray and then concentrating as we pray is sometimes difficult, but God wants to give us the power to do it.

• Turn to page **59** to discover how he wants to help.
• Turn back to page **45** if there are more responsibilities you need to check.

Magazines, mirrors and magnifying glasses!

On page 33 we discovered that the Bible claims to be God's book. All through this book we've been using Bible bits to help us find out facts. We need to discover more and more of what the Bible says.

Anyone who tries to read the Bible soon realises that some bits are easier to understand than others. Everybody has difficulty with parts.

The first problem is trying to work out where to start. There are magazines and booklets to help people find their way around the Bible. Scripture Union publish some of the best. There will be one suitable for you. Ask what is available at church or in a Christian bookshop. If you have difficulty write for advice to: Scripture Union, 130 City Road, London EC1V 2NJ.

Bible reading notes usually give each day a short passage to read from the Bible, then an explanation or a puzzle to complete to help us understand what we have read.

Use a modern translation of the Bible. This book has used the Good News Bible throughout. Another popular one is the New International Version. Try to get hold of one of these.

If you want to read the Bible without study notes start with one of the New Testament books that actually tell the story of Jesus: Matthew, Mark, Luke or John. After you have read a paragraph go back through it and answer some questions.

It may help to think of the Bible as both a mirror and a magnifying glass. Imagine holding a magnifying glass to the page. The type is suddenly bigger.

- Does this Bible bit help explain anything I couldn't see before?
- Does it make God clearer?
- Does it make Jesus easier to understand? Now swap to the mirror. Let's see if you can see yourself in the Bible bit.
- Am I like anyone described in this passage?
- Does it mention anything I should obey or believe or even avoid?

There are many different ways to read the Bible. Try a variety. Find the method that works for you.

Keep a notebook and write down your answers if that helps. Find a convenient time, every day if possible, to read the Bible.

God wants to give us the power to read the Bible because it helps us get to know Jesus better.

• By now you should have finished the list on page **45**. Well done!
• Turn to page **59** to discover how Jesus wants to help.
• If there are more responsibilities you have not yet checked, go back to page **45** and make your choice.

Can I understand the Trinity?

There are some things about God which we can't work out. The Trinity is one such truth. God has shown himself to us as Father, Son and Holy Spirit; three persons, but there is only one God.

When the risen Jesus told his disciples to share his good news with all people, he sent them **'in the name of the Father, the Son and the Holy Spirit'**. (Matthew 28:19). In this Bible bit the word "name" is not plural (that would be names). The Father is not the Son, who is not the Holy Spirit - but there is only God.

This is difficult to understand and puzzles most people. We all know this sum doesn't make sense; 1 + 1 + 1 = 1. But why should we use plus signs? Here's another sum and it does make sense; 1 x 1 x 1 = 1. It helps us understand the Trinity.

H_20 can be water, ice or steam depending on the temperature. They all look very different but they are all made using the same atoms of oxygen and hydrogen. It helps us understand the Trinity.

Father God wants to work in us by his Holy Spirit to make us more like Jesus.

• Turn to page **66** to read about the results of the Spirit's work in our lives (sometimes called the fruit of the Spirit).

Being a Christian

Saying 'yes' to Jesus means we can honestly be called Christians.

Christians know that they are loved by God.

Christians know that he has forgiven them for all their sin.

Christians know that God has given them his Spirit to help them to live his way.

Christians know that they are going to heaven.

They also know that there will still be times when they doubt - rather than have faith.

They will be tempted to do wrong - and sadly will often give in to the temptation.

They know that they have more to learn about life than they have already learnt.

Being a Christian does not mean we have all the answers! It does mean that Jesus lives in us and he's always available.

Before Jesus went back to heaven he said: **"I am with you always"** (Matthew 28:20). In another Bible bit God says: **"I will never leave you; I will never abandon you"** (Hebrews 13:5).

God promises to be our guide through life. That was one of the jobs of a shepherd in Bible times. Psalm 23 is one of the most famous Bible bits that talks about how God will care for us.

If you have said 'yes' to Jesus it would be good to talk

it over with someone who understands. If there are other Christians in your home or family tell them. It may be that you have a special friend you want to share it with. If you belong to a church tell the leaders. If you don't go to church try a few, until you find the one that is right for you. Ask God to show you which one that is.

Well done! I think getting to this page in this book is an achievement.

Keep seeking for answers to the big questions in life.

• Finally turn to page 77.

Your own prayer

On page 51 we discovered that the word STOP is a useful one when making up a prayer. Remember the letters stood for the words:

S: SORRY
T: THANKS
O: OTHERS
P: PERSONAL PLEASE.

It may be helpful to use this as a pattern for your own prayer. Perhaps you could try writing one in rough and then copy it into this space. Remember to be honest. Say what you feel you really need to.

• **Once you have used your prayer turn to page 73.**

Yet more questions!

Well done if you have been honest enough to say that you are not yet ready to say 'yes' to Jesus. He never forces anyone to follow him because it's impossible to bully someone into loving.

Keep up your honesty and openness. Keep asking hard questions. Check out all the big questions in life. Look for answers, both in the Bible and elsewhere. I happen to believe that Christianity makes sense so it has nothing to fear from hard questions. Don't dismiss God's answers just because your friends do. Think things through yourself.

Thank you for working through this book. Now put it on one side. Perhaps come back to it in a few months and see if it begins to make more sense then. Perhaps use a different route through it. One thing is sure. On your search for answers you will need help. Here's one last Bible bit:

"If any of you lacks wisdom he should pray to God, who will give it to him; because God gives generously and graciously to all."

James 1:5

Don't doubt it...just do it...and you'll eventually find the answers.

(P.S. If you just turned to this page to see what it says now go back to page 67 and make another choice!)

An end that isn't the end!

Well done - you've reached the end of this book. (This must be one of the few books where the last page is not the last page!)

Journeying through this book is something like going through life. We started with some big questions.

Can you remember them?

- Who am I?
- Why is this world a mess?
- Are all religions true?

On our journey we've answered some questions - but discovered even more. That experience is going to continue all through our Christian life. We will always have questions. Don't be afraid of questions. Often God asks them to help us discover new truth about ourselves. Don't be afraid to share your questions with others. Don't give up, if answers are hard to find. Look for genuine answers.

Remember what I said on page 7 about other routes through this book. Why not read it another way, using different choices?

As you begin to think more and more about your faith you must:

"let God transform you inwardly by a complete change of mind. Then you will be able to know the will of God - what is good and is pleasing to him and is perfect."

Romans 12:2

Stories in the New Testament

Here are some of the most famous stories about Jesus from the New Testament:

• Birth of Jesus	Luke 2
• Baptism of Jesus	Matthew 3
• Temptation of Jesus	Luke 4
• Calling the disciples	Mark 1
• Sermon on the Mount	Matthew 5, 6 and 7
• Wedding at Cana	John 2
• Nicodemus visits Jesus	John 3
• Stilling the storm	Mark 4
• The twelve disciples	Matthew 10
• Healing a centurion's servant	Luke 7
• Walking on the water	Matthew 14
• The Good Samaritan	Luke 10
• Feeding 5000	John 6
• The Transfiguration	Mark 9
• The lost sheep	Luke 15
• The lost son	Luke 15
• The good shepherd	John 10
• Rich young ruler	Mark 10
• Bartimaeus	Luke 18
• Lazarus	John 11
• Zacchaeus	Luke 19

• Palm Sunday	Mark 11
• The crucifixion	Matthew 26, 27

(see page 22 of this book, but come back to this page!)

• The resurrection	Matthew 28

(see page 36 of this book, but come back to this page!)

Here are some of the famous stories from Acts:

• Ascension	Acts 1
• Pentecost	Acts 2
• Raising a lame man	Acts 3
• Stephen is killed	Acts 7
• Philip and the African	Acts 8
• Saul is converted	Acts 9
• Peter in prison	Acts 12
• Paul at Philippi	Acts 16
• Paul is shipwrecked	Acts 27

• Now go back to page **33** and make another choice.

Stories in the Old Testament

Some of the most famous Bible stories are in the Old Testament. Here's where they can be found:

• Creation	Genesis 1
• Adam and Eve	Genesis 2 and 3
• Noah's Ark	Genesis 6, 7 and 8
• Abraham	from Genesis 12
• Abraham and Isaac	Genesis 22
• Joseph	from Genesis 37
• Moses	from Exodus 2
• Ten Commandments	Exodus 20
• Capture of Jericho	Joshua 6
• Gideon	from Judges 6
• Samson	from Judges 13
• Samuel	from 1 Samuel 1
• David and Goliath	1 Samuel 17
• David and Jonathan	1 Samuel 18, 19 and 20
• Solomon	1 Kings 3
• Elijah	from 1 Kings 17

Other people's stories are found in the book with their name: Ruth, Ezra, Nehemiah, Esther, Isaiah, Jeremiah, Ezekiel, Daniel, Hosea, Jonah.

• Now go back to Page **33** and make another choice.

Why is there suffering in the world?

There is no doubt that Jesus suffered.

An enormous question lots of people ask is:"If there is a God of love why is there so much suffering in the world?"

A big question like this cannot be answered quickly or easily. There are often lots of bits that together make up an answer. Only when all the bits come together will there be a whole answer. It's rather like a jigsaw where eventually a whole picture emerges.

Here are some answer 'bits':

1. Because God allows us to choose, sometimes we choose to hurt other people. So much suffering is caused by wars or drunken drivers or selfish thieves. So often because of a civil war in a country the children in it are starving. This suffering is not God's fault.

2. Sometimes we accidentally hurt people by the mistakes we make. If a car ferry sails without shutting the huge access doors and then capsizes, many families will suffer. Because of human error, others suffer.

3. Sometimes we actually choose to hurt ourselves. When we know that smoking can damage our health, but we carry on doing it, eventually we will suffer.

4. We actually need pain. If you feel ill and go to the doctor you will be asked "Where does it hurt?" If we didn't hurt there would be no warning that our body was not well. By the time we got help we would be much more poorly. At times pain can be seen as a gift from God.

5. Sometimes our stupidity or selfishness causes suffering. We know the earthquake zones of the world, but often ignore this fact when constructing buildings there. It's cheaper to build ones that are not earthquake proof so that's what happens. We know that a volcano may erupt but people still ignore the fact and live too near to it.

These are all bits in the puzzle of suffering. None of them on their own will give an answer, but one thing is sure: when we suffer, God is there with us. He knows what it is to suffer, because Jesus died on the cross.

• If you want to think more about how God is with us when we suffer turn to page **68**.
• If you want to read more about the battle between good and evil turn to page **29**.

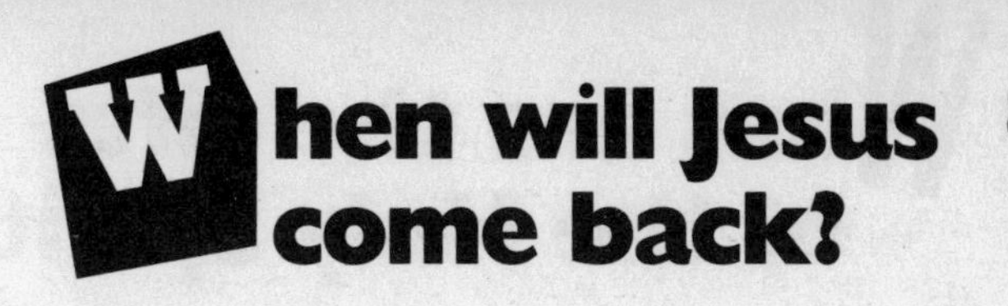

When will Jesus come back?

When our family goes away on holiday, neighbours usually look after the house. We tell Andy and Elaine when we'll be back, so they know to look out for us. I expect your family makes similar arrangements.

The Bible doesn't tell us when Jesus is coming again.

When he was on earth he talked about events that would be signs pointing to it happening. Some would be in the world generally. These include large scale disasters like earthquakes, wars and famines.

Some would be in the church. Christians would be persecuted and hated for their faith. Many people would give up their faith but at the same time the whole world will hear the good news of Jesus.

Jesus tells us that when he returns the sun, moon, and stars will be darkened and he will return in dazzling light with the sound of trumpets. See Matthew 24:29-31.

It will be an incredible world event. But we have nothing to fear if we are friends of Jesus.

• Now either go on to page **64** to read of God's love.
• Or go back to page **43** to investigate other reasons why Jesus' resurrection is so important.

What are the gifts of the Holy Spirit?

God gives us all gifts, but he gives each one different gifts depending on what he wants us to do. These are to be used to build up his church. One Bible bit says:

"There are different kinds of spiritual gifts but the same Spirit gives them."
1 Corinthians 12:4

When we say 'yes' to Jesus he has some gifts for us. He may want us to be a carer; or someone who helps others say 'yes' to Jesus; or someone who helps him cure others; or speak in a language we've never learned; or help plan our church group's programme. There are many more gifts as well.

The Bible has lists of some of these gifts. If you want to look them up they are:

- Romans 12:6-8
- 1 Corinthians 12:8-10
- Ephesians 4:11

None of the gifts are less important than others! People in your church will help you discover your gifts. Ask God to show you what yours are.

• Turn to page **66** to read about the fruit of the Spirit in us.
• Or turn to page **67** and read about saying 'yes' to Jesus.

What is baptism?

John the Baptist was working by the River Jordan. God had given him a job to do. Everyone who was sorry for their sin and wanted a fresh start went into the water - and it was just as if they had a spiritual wash. One day Jesus was baptised by John. You can find the story in Matthew 3:13-17 or Mark 1:9-11.

Jesus' baptism was not because he needed to ask for forgiveness. He identified himself with the rest of us who do!

Nearly all churches still believe that their members should be baptised in water but they vary as to how they do it and who they do it to. Different denominations have different understandings of baptism.

There are two main methods:

1. The christening of babies. Water is either poured or sprinkled over the children. It symbolises the sprinkled blood of Jesus (1 Peter 1:12) on the cross - and that God pours his love into our hearts (Romans 5:5). Christening babies shows that God loves us and accepts us even before we can do anything. The service usually happens around a font in a church.

2. Immersion; sometimes called believer's baptism. This is generally for adults who have already said 'yes' to Jesus. It shows that Christians are united with Jesus in his death, burial and resurrection (Romans 6:3-4). The person being baptised is completely dipped in water. It usually happens in a special tank in the church (called a baptistry) although it sometimes happens in a river, the sea or a swimming pool. This type of baptism allows people to show everyone that they are following Jesus.

Find out how your church baptises people. If you have been christened discover all you can about the event.

When Jesus was baptised, God showed that the Holy Spirit was with him. A dove came and hovered over him. God wants to give us his Holy Spirit too.

• If you have not yet checked all the responsibilities go back to page **45**.
• If you have, go on to page **59**, to read about the Holy Spirit.

What kind of book is the Bible?

The Bible is not a simple book to read. Some parts are easier than others. It is not like a science or history textbook that just teaches about a subject.

In the Bible phrases like, 'God said...' occur thousands of times. The writers believed their message was from God. These words have been tested over the years and God still speaks through them.

Some of God's messages are *prophecies* when he reveals what will happen in the future. In the Old Testament there are over three hundred references to the life of Jesus. These were written hundreds of years before Jesus was born but they all came true. The Bible is reliable.

Other parts of the Bible were written by people who were eye witnesses to actual events. Peter wrote this Bible bit about Jesus;

"We have not depended on made-up stories ... With our own eyes we saw his greatness."

2 Peter 1:16

Christians believe that through the Bible God still speaks to us.

• Turn to page **12** if you want to discover more about the Bible.

• Turn to page **31** if you want to discover other ways that God speaks to us.

What is a miracle?

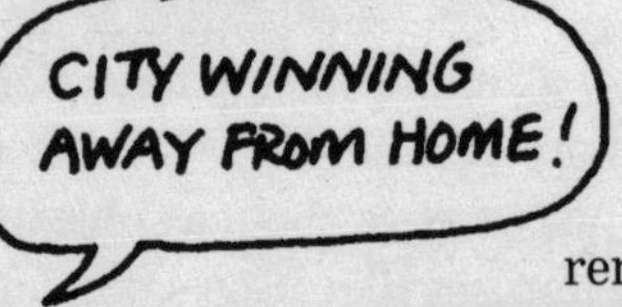

Jesus' life was so remarkable. It seems that whenever he was around miracles happened. Some happened to Jesus, like his birth and coming alive again. Others happened as part of Jesus' dealings with other people. Here's just a selection:

- Turning water into wine at a wedding (John 2:1)
- Walking on water and calming a storm (Matthew 14:22)
- Feeding thousands of people with one boy's picnic (Mark 6:30)
- Raising people from the dead (Luke 8:51)
- Giving sight back to those who were blind (Matthew 9:27)
- Giving a lame man the ability to walk (Matthew 9:1)
- Healing a whole group of people with a skin disease (Luke 17:11)

And there are many more.

A miracle is an amazing event that happens supernaturally. Either it happens more quickly than it would naturally or in a different way to what it would naturally. The Bible sometimes describes miracles as mighty acts of God, or signs and wonders.

Jesus' miracles showed God's power. People realised he was special. The miracles helped them to put their trust in him.

Do miracles still happen?

Miracles happened long before Jesus was on earth. Remember the way the Red Sea opened up and Moses and the Israelites walked through? Or Daniel surviving in a lion's den? Or Jonah in a fish's stomach?

Miracles happened after Jesus had gone back to heaven. His disciples were able to heal people or bring them back from the dead by using the name of Jesus.

God still heals people - sometimes naturally, sometimes supernaturally. We must not limit the ways he can act.

The miracles of Jesus are a sign that he was and is God. He also claimed just that.

Turn to page 38 to discover what he said.

Does God exist?

When it snows, everyone in my family starts acting like very small children. (I'm so old even my children, Lisa and Susie, are grown-up!) We all pull on wellingtons to find the fields of fresh snow. When we get there we want to make the first footprints.

If someone else came along later they would know we existed - because we've left lots of marks.

God has left evidence like footprints all over the universe to show he exists. Here's some evidence:

1. The cosmos is designed brilliantly. There just has to be a creator who made it. Many scientists who study it agree. Don't believe anyone who tells you that belief in God and science can't go together. Many top scientists are Christians.

2. Lots of Christians claim to know God, and he has changed them. He's made selfish people into caring people. He's given people power to live as he wants them to. If he didn't exist he couldn't change people for the better.

3. Every school has a set of rules. At some time, someone sat down and wrote those rules. Within us there is a conscience like a little voice that tells us when we're wrong. Christians believe God first wrote the rules inside us and sets these standards.

4. Christians believe God's biggest footprint in history is the life of Jesus. That's why this book concentrates so much on him. God is obviously very powerful to leave such giant footprints.

• If you would like to meet him turn to page **30**.
• If you think you may be too frightened to meet him turn to page **15**.
• If you want to discover some more about people who don't believe in God turn to page **94**.

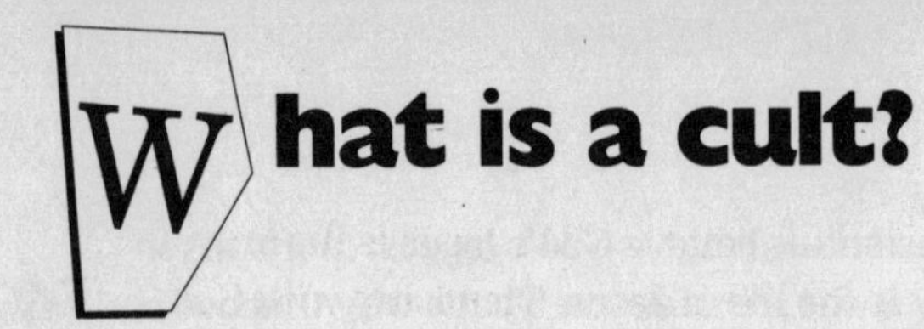

What is a cult?

There are lots of groups that look a bit like a church but are really very different. You may have had Mormons or Jehovah's Witnesses come to your home. You may have heard the Hare Krishna followers, with shaved heads and orange clothes, singing in a shopping precinct. These, and many other groups, are called cults.

The commonest ones are:

- The Jehovah's Witnesses
- The Mormons (or Church of Latter Day Saints)
- The Moonies (or Unification Church)
- Rastafarians
- Transcendental Meditation
- Hare Krishna
- Scientology
- The Unitarian Church

There are many, many more as well.

How are cults different from churches?

If you want to discover if a group is Christian here are three vital points to check. Most cults believe something different on at least one of these:

1. Who is Jesus?

Christians believe that he is one person of the Trinity. He is God the Son.

2. How does God accept us as friends?

Christians believe that faith in Jesus is the only way. There is no way we can earn friendship with God. It is his free gift because of what Jesus did.

3. How do we know the truth?

Christians believe the Bible is the one and only book that can be called God's written word. No one person can be trusted to interpret or explain it all. Cults often have other "sacred" books, or just trust one person's ideas.

When Jesus was on earth he warned his followers of "false prophets (who) will appear and deceive many people" (Matthew 24:11).

Beware of any group that wants to tell you what to think! What a difference from this book where you have to think for yourself!

• Turn back to page **57** and make another choice!

Either 'yes' or 'no'

Do you have staff training days at school? All the pupils have a day off but the teachers have to work. It's not always clear which days are holidays and you might argue about it in the playground.

"Monday is a day off."

"No, it's not. We've got to come to school."

The difference may go on all lunchtime. You might say:

"Perhaps it is a holiday. Perhaps it's not."

Eventually someone finds a teacher - and the argument ends. The answer has to be either 'yes' or 'no.'

Some people don't know whether God exists or not. They are called agnostics (pronounced ag-nos-tics). Like our playground argument the answer has to be either 'yes' or 'no.' A real agnostic has to keep looking for the answer to the question "Is there a God?" You can't stay agnostic.

Atheists (Ay-thee-ists) say God doesn't exist. They have made up their minds. It is very difficult to say for certain that all the evidence points to no God.

Christians believe there is lots of evidence. God has announced his existence in the Bible.

• Let's discover more about it. Turn to page **33**.

What's in a name?

When my mum was expecting me my sister told everyone she was going to have a baby sister called John! Have you ever discovered what your first name means? John means "a gift from God".

Names were even more important in Bible times because they said something about the person. By looking at the names given to Jesus we discover lots about who he was. There are so many names given to him in the Bible we've only got space to check out the really popular ones.

JESUS: This is a common Jewish name and actually means saviour. The angel who told Joseph of the birth of Christ said "you will name him Jesus because he will save his people from their sins" (Matthew 1:21).

CHRIST: The Greek word means someone who has been anointed (had a few drops of oil poured on them). This was the mark of a priest whose job was to bring God to people and people to God.

MESSIAH: The specially-anointed person promised by God in the Old Testament. The Jews expected him to be their rescuer. Jesus widened that to include anyone.

LORD: The word really means the teacher whom I'm obeying and making my master.

With names like these it is obvious Jesus was someone very special.

• Turn to page **16** and begin to discover who Jesus is.

Index

Because of the type of book this is, some of the subjects start on the page listed but then run over to others, depending on the decision you make!!